SHOOTING STARS

Book 4

TROUBLE FOR THE GIRLS!

Created by Mick Waters and Wendy Bloom

Illustrated by Patricia Ludlow

Written by Wendy Bloom
Adapted by Marie Birkinshaw
Designed by Keith Grady

You can read all about the Shooting Stars:

Book 1: ***Fireworks Fiasco***
Book 2: ***Laslo's Boots***
Book 3: ***Lights Out!***
Book 4: ***Trouble for the Girls!***
Book 5: ***Own Goal***
Book 6: ***Football on the Farm***

With appreciation to children in Birmingham schools, especially the Year 6 pupils at Brookfield School, Birmingham for their advice

Birmingham Advisory & Support Service
BASS

Birmingham City Council

Published in 2005 by Birmingham Advisory and Support Service, Balden Road, Harborne, Birmingham B32 2EH

Project Co-ordinator: Fran Stevens
Editors: Marie Birkinshaw and Shirley Jackson
Design: Keith Grady
Football Consultant: Ian Thomas

ISBN No. 1-905182-06-6

In Book 1, we learned how six very different children, who are all equally crazy about football, became friends through the City School Thursday football practice. They started meeting to play football at the rec at the back of Lily's house every Saturday morning. They did lots of things together, and decided to form their own club – The Shooting Stars Club.

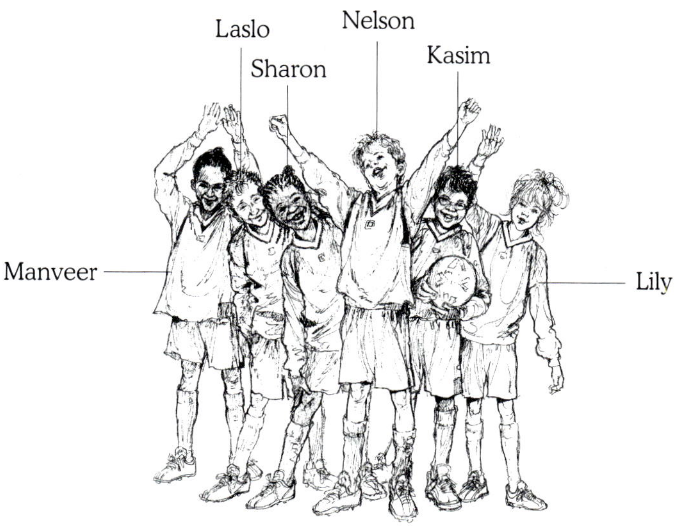

On bonfire night, Kasim was knocked unconscious trying to rescue the Club's charter from a burning shed. Luckily he was rescued by Lily's mum, and all was well.

In Book 2, we followed the school's and the Club's football practice through November and December. A football talent scout watched the players and Laslo was chosen to play in a Youth Team Trial Match. All the Shooting Stars helped with his training – but they wished that he could buy a brand new pair of football boots which they could not afford. Laslo was bullied about his old boots by an opposing team player at the Trial Match. But a new friend Jitesh stood up for Laslo and they played some amazing football. Meanwhile, preparations were in hand for the Winter Concert at school. Despite illness, Sharon sang superbly and was noticed by a TV producer. On the last Saturday before Christmas, the Shooting Stars were in a local Sports Shop and noticed some teenagers acting suspiciously. Their quick action led to the arrest of the two thieves. Laslo got some brand new boots as a reward and all the Shooting Stars got new scarves.

In Book 3, Lily hated the thought of having to spend Christmas with her dad and his new family. But it didn't go as badly as she feared. She joined the Shooting Stars on Boxing Day for the Inter-Schools Pre-match where there was lots of excitement in store. Then she watched the Big Match with her dad and the family. Lily came to the rescue when the lights went out and the baby started to choke. We left the six Shooting Stars looking forward to the New Year.

Chapter 1

It was February and the City School's football team had done well in the Inter-Schools' League since the New Year. They were now in third position and were in fact the only mixed team in the top eight. It was rare that anyone from the Shooting Stars was missed from the team selection. They were always there for after-school practice on Thursdays, for matches and, of course, for Saturday mornings at Lily's Place. Did I say all of them? Well, not quite… Laslo sometimes had to play for the Youth Team and couldn't always be there. Since Jitesh had stood up for him in the first trial match, they had become firm friends and were playing really well together in the team.

Laslo's English was also getting much better. He could join in with all the team talk now and even with some of their odd jokes:

What do you call a wolf who referees football matches?

A fair wolf.

The Shooting Stars often talked about the famous Pre-match on Boxing Day, especially as, being a small school, they'd won against all the odds. They still laughed when they remembered the sky divers coming down in the wrong place on the pitch and then the lights going out.

But football wasn't their only talk. There had also been lots to say about Sharon's TV audition that had been held in January.

It had been pretty scary with loads of girls and boys signed up to sing. Sharon had had to wait for ages too. Then she was taken into the room where they did all the recording. There were a couple of men with a wall of screens and sliding buttons and there had been vast amounts of amplification equipment lying around. Sharon had had to do her singing wearing earphones in a tiny booth.

It had been great fun though and, even better, she had recently heard that she'd been shortlisted as a singer for their future productions.

"What did your mum and dad say about it?" asked Nelson.

"Dad went a bit OTT. He thinks it's much better for a girl to do singing than play football. He's started calling me his 'Singing Star'. But Mum doesn't agree, she wants me to be a famous woman footballer, so she calls me her 'Shooting Star'. It's getting so uncool, as they are always talking about it to other people. And to make matters worse they've both started saying that I'll have to make up my mind soon and choose between them. They say I'll be too busy to do both and not be able to do my school work properly."

Lily gave her a hug, "Don't worry, it's all down to you in the end."

"Yeah, I know," said Sharon, "and I'm going to keep doing both while I can."

Chapter 2

It was break time on a wet Wednesday morning. They were all together except for Kasim. (His family and the Muslim community were celebrating Eid. Most of the Muslim children had one or two days off school during that time.)

Manveer was flicking through a local paper that one of the teachers had left lying on a desk. Suddenly a headline caught his eye. "Listen up!" he called out, "You'll never believe this!"

Manveer read out the headline.

"GIRLS BANNED FROM INTER-SCHOOLS SOCCER SEMI-FINALS!"

The Shooting Stars were stunned.
"What's that?" asked Lily.
"I'll read it out," said Manveer.

GIRLS BANNED FROM INTER-SCHOOL SOCCER SEMI-FINALS!

Our sports reporter has found out that the Inter-Schools' Football Committee has rejected the idea of including girls in what was always an all-male competition. The experiment to allow mixed teams in the last two years has not brought forward as many female players as hoped so it has been decided to go back to making the final stages of this series a boys-only competition. Money would be put into girls-only football next year to try to encourage more girls to play.

In an interview with the Ferris School squad, winners of last year's Inter-Schools' League trophy, the boys stated that they were in agreement with the decision.

"We don't think that having girls in matches is a good idea. They can't play as well as the boys and they make a fuss if they get tackled too hard."

Sharon exploded, "How can they say such a thing? What was that Committee thinking about? Mixed teams work really well. Small schools like City School would never have enough girls wanting to play serious football to make it worth having a girls-only team."

Manveer looked at Sharon. "And you're as tough and fast as any boy. I'd try not to get tackled by you if I was in the opposition!"

"And Lily never makes a fuss," went on Nelson. "Do you remember when Sam fouled you in the penalty area? You just got up and scored the goal!"

The five Shooting Stars couldn't wait for break to end. They were all agreed… something had to be done.

They would certainly have plenty to say to Mrs Cox when they found her. They were sure they would have her full support, even if she did play regularly for the local women's-only team.

Chapter 3

The Shooting Stars managed to find Mrs Cox and Mr Foster at lunchtime. They were shocked to read the news. But both of them said that the six children would need to wait to see what the new Head, Mr di Paolo, had to say about it before they were prepared to comment any more.

Mr di Paolo would not be back in school until the following morning. (Mrs Mizzen had left the school at Christmas to become an adviser.)

Sharon and the others weren't so sure about Mr di Paolo. They still hadn't got used to him yet. He seemed too young to be a Head Teacher and he didn't seem to be even half as approachable as Mrs Mizzen had been.

Nevertheless, they all got to school early on Thursday morning and met up outside the Head's office. At least Kasim was back and they had been able to get in touch and tell him the problem the previous evening.

"Come on in. I have to see some parents in five minutes, so you'll need to be quick."

Kasim stepped forward. He told the Head about the newspaper article.

Mr di Paolo looked serious. "I hadn't heard anything about this. I'll try to talk to Mr Foster and Mrs Cox at break time and we'll try to see what's going on."

"But you will do something about it, won't you?" pleaded Sharon. Her voice had gone a bit higher. "It's discriminating against the City School and it's sexist!"

"Well, it's not strictly sexist, when they promise to do something about girls' football. But let's find out more about it before we get too excited, shall we?"

The Shooting Stars left the office. They were not at all happy. They were not even sure that Mr di Paolo was really on the case.

In the practice after school, the Shooting Stars tried to talk to the rest of the football squad about the ban on girls. But they soon found that not all the squad were as concerned as they were. Shushan hadn't been chosen to play in the team this term, and nor had two of the other girls. They didn't seem keen to back the Shooting Stars up as much as Sharon had expected. They rather liked the idea of a girls' squad, even though nothing would happen until September.

Sharon was disgusted and told them so.

"But what about the City School team in the League this year," she stormed. "Girls are meant to be like sisters here. We're meant to be solid together. You're traitors!"

The next morning a note came round the classes from Mrs Cox saying that there would be an emergency meeting for the football squad at dinner break. They all knew by now what this would be about.

Dinnertime came and the whole squad gathered in Mrs Cox's classroom. Everyone went silent when the two teachers came in.

Mrs Cox began, "OK, sit down everyone. This is a big shock. We have been in touch with the football committee. They say that the newspaper was right. It had apparently always been planned that the inclusion of mixed teams in the Inter-School League would be an experiment. A review had also always been planned to take place before the finals games got underway because of strong pressure for boys-only teams. Very few schools have submitted mixed teams for this trophy and in fact we're the only team remaining. They say there are other trophies that mixed teams can compete for other than this one this year, and they say that the decision is final."

Mr Foster joined in, "We're so sorry. We had no idea that this was going to happen when we submitted the team for this trophy. It is a shame for our current line-up, but I'm sure that we have sufficient boys that are good enough to play and that City School should still be able to compete for the trophy this year. It's a pity too that we're too late to enter a mixed team into any other of the competitions. Sorry, girls. You'll have to wait for your turn next year."

Immediately the whole squad started talking.

"It's not fair!"

"We should have known about it!"

"We've got enough good boy players, we can manage without the girls."

"Girls are getting into everything these days, my mum says it's bad."

The Shooting Stars couldn't take it any longer. They'd already decided on a joint plan of action. They stood up together.

Everyone stopped talking… all eyes were fixed on them.

Nelson started. "OK. Well… this is how we see it. We either drop Sharon and Lily from the team… and we four boys drop out as well… or we start a campaign to change people's minds. At least we can raise it at the School Council to see what the whole school think, can't we?"

"Well, yes, we can certainly do that," considered Mrs Cox. "And without any of the Shooting Stars, I can see that the City School team this year would be at a particular disadvantage."

"I read that women's football is the fastest growing sport in Britain," said someone at the back, meaning to be helpful. "So they should have their own league and not be in mixed teams!"

Sharon turned round quickly to see who said it. A group of boys, not usually in the team, looked uneasy. She decided not to say anything. She would wait until the School Council meeting next week… and she would certainly have something to say then, since she was a School Council representative… and they had other plans in hand too.

Chapter 4

Mondays, after school, was the school band practice. City School was practising for an inter-schools concert to be held in a big hall in the middle of the city in a few weeks' time.

As it happened, Lily and Sharon were both key players in the band. Sharon played trumpet and Lily played trombone. Most of the band were there already when the girls turned up. Some of the band members (girls and boys) came up to them to say how sorry they were about the match ban.

"It's not over yet!" muttered Sharon

Mr Mayo came in at that moment.

"OK, let's get straight into it, we haven't got much time now and we still have some way to go. Practice makes perfect, as they say. We'll start with the Military March."

The band all stood up ready to play… not quite all, though. Sharon and Lily stayed sitting silently, side by side.

Mr Mayo didn't notice and raised his baton. Now, the music should have started with a short trumpet solo from Sharon, but when Mr Mayo waved his arms in the air, no sound came. He tapped on the music stand.

"Sharon, pay attention, we can't start this piece without you!"

Everyone turned round and looked at Sharon, sitting silently with Lily.

"Sharon! What's the matter with you?"

"Sorry, Mr Mayo, but if girls can't play in the football match with boys this year, then they won't play in a mixed band concert either. At least me and Lily won't."

Mr Mayo stretched his hands above his head and thought for a moment. "Mmm, I thought that decision would spell trouble. Are all you other girls happy to play by any chance?"

There were ten other girls in the band, trumpet, cornet and drummers. They exchanged looks quickly. Two of Lily's friends sat down and put their instruments on the floor. Two of Sharon's friends did the same. Then the other six followed their lead. The boys looked on, unsure what to do or say.

"Then I declare this music practice is over," said Mr Mayo, picking up his papers. "Two wrongs don't make a right, you know. But I wish you luck in your campaign. I agree it does seem a bit unfair."

Sharon and Lily soon found the other four Shooting Stars and told them that everything was going according to plan. Word was getting round fast. Most of the pupils and staff seemed keen to keep a mixed team playing in this year's Inter-Schools League. It was the first year that City School had done so well, and everyone was worried that changing to a boys-only team would spoil their chances – especially if none of the Shooting Stars played.

Then everything happened at double speed.

The Head met with the school council at which Sharon made a long speech in support of this year's mixed team. It was agreed that they would support the girls...

THEN

an emergency meeting of the school governors was called. They agreed that the school should object to the ban on girls playing in this year's match...

THEN

the Shooting Stars got in touch with the local MP to ask for her to help them get the ban dropped...

THEN

the local press came to school, took photos and wrote an article supporting the girls...

THEN

all the football club made placards and wore badges:
"Equal Rights for Girl Footballers!" and "Football Fairness"...

AND THEN

a School Representative and the Head were invited to an open meeting of the Inter-Schools' Football Committee, which would take place the following week.

The Shooting Stars were on a such a high after their progress so far, that it was not surprising that they had forgotten about Shrove Tuesday (Pancake Day).

After school, Sharon's mum invited all the Stars round for pancakes. They took it in turns to toss them. Laslo's got stuck on top of the cupboard, but he still got it down and ate it!

"I'm stuffed... and we're doing it again later with my cousins!" gasped Sharon.

In fact Sharon had been so busy that she had nearly forgotten about the promise of future singing at the TV studios.

Then just when she wasn't expecting it, the phone rang and it was the TV producer who was offering her a chance to sing in a chorus for a musical. The practices would be on Wednesdays starting next week. Sharon's dad was really keen for her to attend. But Sharon knew that she would have to say no. She couldn't go to the essential first practice next Wednesday. That was the day the Football Committee would be meeting and she had been chosen as the pupil representative to go with Mr di Paolo. So it was, with only a glimmer of regret, that she declined the offer and risked kissing goodbye to her chances for singing success.

Chapter 5

The big meeting day came all too quickly. The Head and Sharon weren't the only ones at the meeting – two press people, a photographer and a journalist were there, too. There was also a tall, young, distinguished-looking woman, who Sharon noticed was wearing a lapel badge. It was shaped like a football.

Sharon looked around the walls of the council room. There were dozens of photos of football teams going back over a hundred years or more. And all the pictures and team photos were of men!

Then the five committee members filed in and they were all men too!

The chairman started the proceedings.

"I have called this meeting, due to public pressure, to discuss the ban on mixed teams in the forthcoming Inter-Schools Football finals. You all know the arguments. I'm sure that you have seen the TV and press reports. We will start with discussion from the committee members and then throw it open to our visitors."

The debate began slowly going to and fro between the committee.

One elderly man argued fiercely against girls playing football at all. "In my day girls would never have thought of playing football. They played netball and were happy with that. But now they have their own Leagues and they are best kept separate from the start. Mixed football is too tough for girls, it's too physical and they will get hurt."

Sharon tried to jump to her feet and was going to interrupt, but Mr di Paolo pulled her back down to the bench. "Wait, Sharon, you'll get your turn!"

The discussions continued even more slowly and Sharon began to get bored.

Then at long last the chairman stood up and looked around.

"I know that we have one of the pupils here from the school leading the campaign. Perhaps, you'd like to talk to the Committee now."

Mr di Paolo nodded to Sharon. She took a deep breath and stood up as tall as she could and began.

"I am one of the Shooting Stars Club, Sir. We are four boys and two girls. We made ourselves into a club to play football and we have a charter that says we are all equal. We practise football whenever we can and we really help each other to give our best to the game. Our school, City School, isn't big enough to compete with both a boys' and a girls' squad for any trophies. But we do have an outstanding mixed football team, of which I'm proud to be a member. I couldn't have learnt half as much about football or practised half as much without this chance to play in a mixed team. We want the opportunity to compete for this year's trophy because we have worked really hard for it."

She sat down, her face was all hot and her pulse was racing. Mr di Paolo congratulated her and she even got some applause.

"Anyone else?" asked the Chairman.

Chapter 6

There was a pause, then the mystery woman stood up.

"I am the captain of the England women's football team. I would like the committee to see a short extract from our recent video of the last finals match against France. I wish to point out that the majority of women in our current team played in mixed teams when they were children."

The video extract showed a fast-moving game. The players were skilled and played good, clean football. The captain switched off the TV at the end of the footage. She faced the row of members, and said, "I urge the committee to encourage girls to play at every opportunity – especially alongside boys at primary school where they can learn skills and become good footballers like the current team. To deny them this opportunity will risk turning away many potentially very competent players."

"Thank you," said the Chairman. "We will take a vote on it."

There was a tense silence whilst the five committee members made their votes, and the decision was taken.

"The committee have voted 4 – 1 in favour of girls being allowed to play in this competition," said the Chairman. "Can I add my own good wishes to the City School football team!"

Sharon bent her head down, fearing that everyone would see her tears of joy. Then when she looked up, she was surprised to see Mr di Paolo shaking hands with the England Captain. They were talking like old friends. "I'm glad you were able to get here. Come and meet Sharon." Mr di Paolo explained that they had been friends at university. He had asked for the captain's support when he heard about the troubles of the mixed team. And, even better, she would be coming into the school to talk to the children.

***

The next day it seemed that the whole school was celebrating the wonderful news. "Now all we have to do is win," said Mr di Paolo in Assembly. What a thought!

The children learned in the same Assembly that it was the Chinese New Year. Mr di Paolo explained that there are 12 animals in the Chinese Zodiac and each one has a year given over to it.

"Taking it in turns the animals include:

rat, ox, tiger, hare,
dragon, snake, horse, sheep,
monkey, fowl, dog, pig.

The new year is fixed by a lunar calendar and comes between 1st January and 19th February in the western world."

"Very tricky!" whispered Lily.

"Not if you know how to work it out," Manveer whispered back.

Mr di Paolo also explained even more! "The celebrations could last three days with fire crackers being set off on Chinese new year's eve. Chinese children wear new clothes and also have lots of sweetmeats, made out of sticky rice."

Shushan had now patched things up with Sharon and had invited her to sleep over and share her family's Chinese New Year celebrations.

Shushan explained: "We call this 'Spring Festival' and it's the oldest and most important festival because we celebrate the Earth coming back to life after winter. The year you are born in has an effect on your personality – monkeys, like my dad, are mischievous!

"Mum has been working really hard to get ready. Before we can celebrate anything, we clean the house right through, we have our hair cut and buy new clothes."

Sharon liked the bit about new clothes, but wasn't so sure about all the cleaning.

"What's that all about?" asked Sharon, looking at the red banners hanging from the front door.

"We've been painting Chinese characters onto red paper for good luck. Red is our lucky colour – you're going to see a lot of it about."

Shushan's mum opened the door, "Quick, come in, come in," she called. "We have to shut the doors and windows to keep our good luck in." Sharon stepped into the house and was immediately transported by the bustle of smells, colours and sounds: incense, cooking and a house full of chatter and laughter.

When they all sat down to eat, Shushan's dad gave the children a red envelope with money in it. "Kung hei fat choy!" he said. "Happy New Year!" The food was delicious – sticky rice sweets, steamed dumplings and fried crescent-shaped parcels. Sharon had never had a meal like it. And she had no trouble in staying up until midnight to watch the fireworks.

On New Year's Day, more excitement was planned as Shushan and Sharon were meeting up with the rest of the Shooting Stars to see the dragon dance. They all wore something new and Shushan's family took them into the city centre.

Laslo jumped as a firecracker exploded nearby – he had to think where he was – a bang like that meant something very different in Kosovo.

The noise was incredible. Wherever they looked, there were people cheering and shouting, calling the dragon to come their way. The dragon moved through the crowds accompanied by a throbbing drum beat that rolled and paused as the dragon climbed and dipped.

"This atmosphere is amazing," said Nelson, "but why is the dragon eating cabbages?"

"There are red envelopes with lucky messages and money inside the cabbages," said Shushan. "The dragon eats the cabbage and the money, then spits the cabbage out. The green leaves mean that that business will make a lot of money and have good luck."

Chapter 7

Before long, the day of the big semi-final match dawned. It was bright but cold. The team had been drawn against the Ferris School – the very boys that the Shooting Stars particularly wanted to beat. In fact the whole pride of City School seemed to be resting on the shoulders of the Shooting Stars, especially on the girls.

Sharon woke up very early with a sick, excited feeling in her stomach. This was it! "Today or never!" she thought.

"Special breakfast for my Shooting Star!" her mum said as she came down into the kitchen. Sharon looked at the large plate of sausage, egg and bacon.

"I can't eat that. I'll be sick!" she said.

She ended up having orange juice and taking a sausage sandwich to school for break.

"You can always go back to singing, if you lose," said her dad. Sharon didn't appreciate the joke.

The squad got together for lunch and a team briefing. Things weren't looking too good. Laslo had been picked at the same time for an important Youth Match and wouldn't be playing for City School that day. The Stars and the school understood that this was a big chance for him, and wouldn't let him back out.

The Inter-Schools match was to be held at a school outside the city that was neutral ground. A bus took the squad and some supporters there and they arrived with plenty of time. A passing shower of rain meant that play wouldn't be easy.

"We'll show that Ferris team not to keep girls out of football!" said Sharon and she took Lily's hand as they ran out onto the pitch for the warm-up.

The match began...

It was even at first, both teams were good at attacking and defending. There was some serious football, but no goals.

Then Nelson built up an attack, passing the ball slickly out onto the wing.

One of the Ferris team intercepted the ball and passed it to the centre forward. Sharon lunged in front to tackle the player, but she slipped on the wet grass!

The centre forward scored a brilliant goal!!

"Told you we could beat the girls! Now she'll start crying," the Ferris centre forward sneered.

Sharon wished that she could die... but she certainly wasn't going to cry. She got stuck in again and got on with the game, no more mistakes. But today she knew she wasn't playing her best, and the City attackers weren't fairing much better either.

At half time the score was still 1 – 0 to the Ferris school.

Mrs Cox had a word with Sharon and took her off at half time, putting on an extra attacker. They were really missing Laslo. The team carried on without her and she was left, wrapping herself up with a spare track suit on the touch line. Sharon felt she had let everyone down. Had it all been worth fighting for?

The Ferris team were not past playing dirty. But the referee spotted them. Soon the first free kick of the match came up… Manveer took his spot, the rest of the City team were on their toes, ready. He kicked a strong, curving ball towards goal. The team surged forward like an attacking army, the goalie went the wrong way and the ball ended up in the corner of the net.

“GOAL!!” Sharon threw off the layers wrapped around her and cheered really loudly.

One-All… but not for long. Another foul, this time on Lily. She was angry now, and took advantage of another free kick, which she blasted across the pitch.

Manveer came up quickly and kicked high. Lily then ran under the ball again and, all the others raced towards the goal.

But Lily didn't need help. She kicked straight and true into the back of the net.

GOAL NUMBER TWO!

There was no more drama and the game ended with City School the clear winners, 2 – 1.

Chapter 8

For the moment, the jubilant team seemed to forget about Sharon and she settled herself sadly at the side. The goalie from the Ferris team came off the pitch quietly, head down. He sat down beside Sharon.

"Those free kicks freaked me out!" he muttered miserably.

"Yeah?" replied Sharon.

"You get so worked up, you can't play like you do in practices," he mumbled.

Sharon knew how he felt. "Ah well, my dad says it's only a game."

Neither of them believed that – boy or girl! But they also knew they'd get over it and soon be playing well again.

The Sunday after the match was Mothers' Day. Sharon was due to sing a solo in her church. She had invited Lily to come, but now she felt like backing out.

"I know I'll mess up, just like the football," she moaned. "And I haven't been practising half as much as I should have been."

To make things worse, the local radio station who had heard Sharon sing at the TV auditions had rung Sharon's home and spoken to her dad. He'd agreed to speak to the pastor to see if they could record Sharon's solo in the church for live-broadcasting on Mothers' Day.

"But that's great, isn't it?" asked Lily. "Remember the applause at the Christmas concert?"

"I s'pose." They talked for a time – Lily trying to support her best friend.

In the event, Sharon sang her solo brilliantly. The song was broadcast live and it was stunning. She was surrounded by the congregation afterwards. Both her dad and her mum were proud of her and so was Lily.

The performance was all the talk when they next met up with the Shooting Stars.

"I wonder if you will be a famous singer or a famous football star," said Kasim.

"I *do* love singing," said Sharon. "But I've made up my mind, I'm going to be the first black women's Captain for England!"

Lily drew a letter out of her track suit pocket.

"Talking of the England Women's Team Captain – Mr di Paolo gave this to me yesterday. I'd forgotten all about it."

She read out loud:

To the Shooting Stars,

Many congratulations on winning the Inter-Schools Match. I am delighted for you all.

Please accept these free tickets for the next Women's England match with my compliments. Keep playing the greatest game of all.

Yours sincerely,

Janice

To be continued in Book 5:
Own Goal!

"READ ALL ABOUT OUR FAIRNESS CAMPAIGN"

What makes a successful campaign?

The City School campaign was successful because they followed some simple rules. They *decided what they wanted to achieve and did their homework!*

First Sharon was very clear about what she wanted the committee to think about. She made three key points:

- there should be equality for all members of the school football team;
- the school is not big enough to have a separate boys' team and a separate girls' team; and
- the team has worked very hard in the tournament with the girls contributing as much as the boys.

Talking to people and getting organised

Sharon knew she had the support of the teachers because she had talked to them. She was well organised in getting people on her side who had the power to change things: School Council, the governors, the MP and the local newspaper. All this activity meant that the Inter-Schools' Football Committee couldn't ignore the problem.

Making good contacts

By talking to the press and their MP, the Shooting Stars and the school were able to keep their campaign in the spotlight. They were able to focus on the key issue – that the team was being discriminated against because it had girls in it.

What I learnt from the campaign

When I first heard that mixed teams were going to be excluded, I was really angry about it. I called the girls who didn't support me 'traitors' but now I know that wasn't fair.

Lily and I decided not to play our instruments in the band because this would show other pupils and teachers who weren't involved in football how strongly we felt about it. Mr Mayo was right when he said that "two wrongs don't make a right". I think it was OK to make the point once, but we didn't want to spoil the chances for the whole band because our chances in the football team had been spoilt. We needed the band to support us not to hate us for stopping them playing, too.

Help from the whole school

The school did a lot to help us – the teachers didn't like us being disqualified from the competition when we had got so far. The School Council was a brilliant place to look for proper support from the school. I learnt a lot about putting across my argument from doing that. The governors also supported us, because the School Council felt that it was important.

I felt very let down when the other girls didn't back me up, but we only changed people's minds when we talked to them clearly and calmly.

Building a fair society

The things we take for granted like free healthcare, state education, clean water, democracy and equal rights for all people regardless of gender, age, disability, race, nationality or culture, have not always been here. Men and women have campaigned over many years, and some have even sacrificed their lives, to make our lives fairer. Today, much of this work is continued by government-funded bodies because it is only when we work together for things that we truly believe in that we will achieve them.

The Equal Opportunities Commission

www.eoc.org.uk

Women. Men. Different. Equal.
Equal Opportunities Commission

The EOC believes in a society where men and women are treated equally. They campaign for men and women:

- to have the same chances at work and to be paid the same money for doing the same job;
- to feel that they can work in any industry;
- to share the responsibility for looking after the home, children or elderly or sick relatives;
- to be equally likely to be in positions of authority and responsibility;
- to be safe from violence at home and outside.

The Commission for Racial Equality

www.cre.gov.uk

COMMISSION FOR RACIAL EQUALITY

The CRE campaigns for a fair and just society that values the differences between people from different racial, national and cultural backgrounds and that gives everyone an equal chance to work, learn and live without discrimination, prejudice and racism.

The Disability Rights Commission

www.drc-gb.org.uk

Disability Rights Commission

The DRC goal is to build a society where all disabled people can participate fully as equal citizens. This means that disabled people can live, work, travel and enjoy a social life just as easily as people without a disability.

British Youth Council
www.byc.org.uk

British Youth Council

BYC aims to

- provide a voice for young people;
- promote equality for young people;
- help young people to become more involved in decisions that affect their lives;
- advance young people's participation in society and civic life.

To find out more, consult:
www.childrensworld.org

World's Children's Prize for the Rights of the Child